{IT CHANGED THE WORLD}

INVENTION OF
ROBOTICS

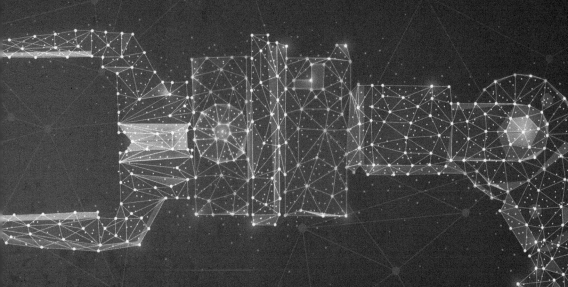

Robin Koontz

ROurke
Educational Media
rourkeeducationalmedia.com

A Division of
Carson
Dellosa
Education

BEFORE AND DURING READING ACTIVITIE

Before Reading: *Building Background Knowledge and Vocabulary*

Building background knowledge can help children process new information and build upon what they already know. Before reading a book, it is important to tap into what children already know about the topic. This will help them develop their vocabulary and increase their reading comprehension.

Questions and Activities to Build Background Knowledge:

1. Look at the front cover of the book and read the title. What do you think this book will be about?
2. What do you already know about this topic?
3. Take a book walk and skim the pages. Look at the table of contents, photographs, captions, and bold words. Did these text features give you any information or predictions about what you will read in this book?

Vocabulary: *Vocabulary Is Key to Reading Comprehension*

Use the following directions to prompt a conversation about each word.

- Read the vocabulary words.
- What comes to mind when you see each word?
- What do you think each word means?

Vocabulary Words:

- artificial intelligence
- automaton
- autonomous
- hazardous
- humanoid
- hydraulics
- industrial
- infrared
- mythology
- robotics

During Reading: *Reading for Meaning and Understanding*

To achieve deep comprehension of a book, children are encouraged to use close reading strategies. During reading, it is important to have children stop and make connections. These connections result in deeper analysis and understanding of a book.

Close Reading a Text

During reading, have children stop and talk about the following:

- Any confusing parts
- Any unknown words
- Text to text, text to self, text to world connections
- The main idea in each chapter or heading

Encourage children to use context clues to determine the meaning of any unknown words. These strategies will help children learn to analyze the text more thoroughly as they read.

When you are finished reading this book, turn to the next-to-last page for Text-Dependent Questions and an Extension Activity.

TABLE OF CONTENTS

ROBOTICS IN HISTORY

Have you seen movies about robots? Have you heard about them dancing, driving cars, or making things? A robot is a mechanical device that can perform tasks done by humans. Some are remote-controlled and need humans to direct them. Others are **autonomous**, which means they operate on their own. This second kind of robot is called an **automaton**.

DEFIANT ROBOTS

The word *robot* was first used to describe mechanical devices in 1921. It was in a Czechoslovakian play about mechanical men working in factory assembly lines. In it, the robots rebel against their human masters.

A security robot patrols the parking lot of a Samsung office building, keeping the employees safe.

An autonomous robot can power itself, control its movements, and sense its surroundings. Both remote-controlled and autonomous robots can take on tasks too difficult, too dangerous, or just too boring for people to do.

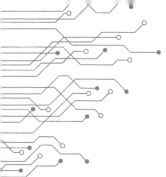

Robotics is much older than you might think. Inventors started thinking about automatons thousands of years ago. The idea was mentioned in classical **mythology** and ancient legends. In ancient times, people constructed clocks and statues that could move using **hydraulics**.

This was before computers or even electricity!

This water clock is from the late fifth century BCE.
Water dripped out of it slowly. You could tell time
by looking at how much water was left inside.

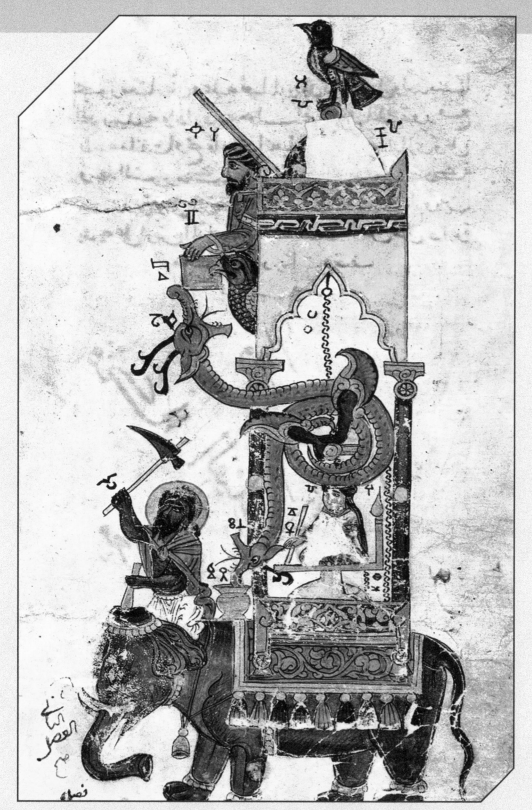

The inventor Al-Jazari, born in 1136, designed an elephant clock featuring automatons striking cymbals and a robotic chirping bird.

In the late 1550s CE, an inventor named Juanelo Turriano built an automaton called Lute Player Lady. It stepped, strummed a lute, and turned its head back and forth.

These unique devices and many others were just the beginning for robotics. By the middle of the 20th century, robots had already begun to change the world.

David Roentgen created this automaton in 1874 for Queen Marie Antoinette. It plays an instrument called a dulcimer.

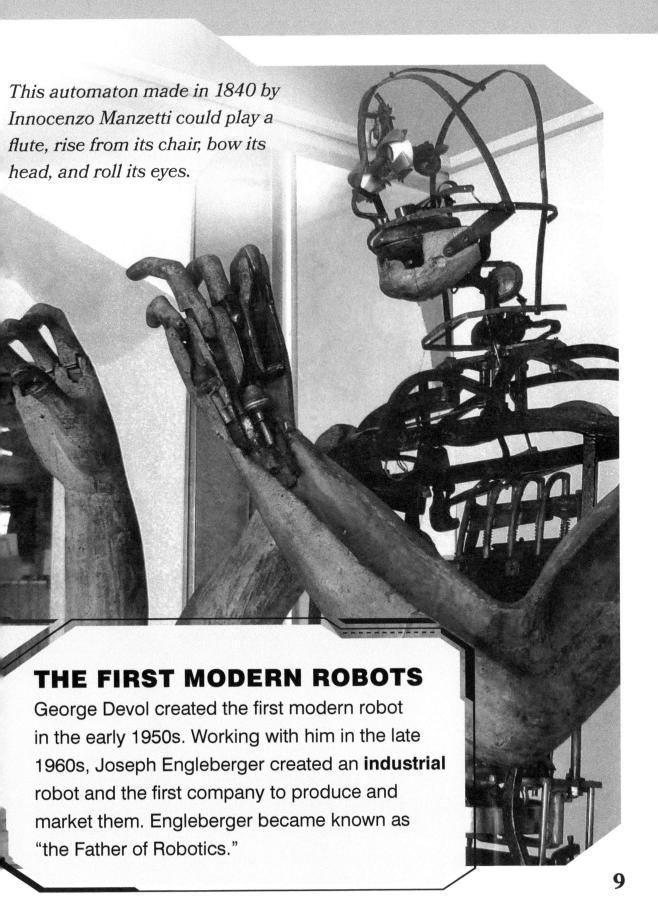

This automaton made in 1840 by Innocenzo Manzetti could play a flute, rise from its chair, bow its head, and roll its eyes.

THE FIRST MODERN ROBOTS

George Devol created the first modern robot in the early 1950s. Working with him in the late 1960s, Joseph Engleberger created an **industrial** robot and the first company to produce and market them. Engleberger became known as "the Father of Robotics."

MANUFACTURING AND FARMING ROBOTS

Perhaps you have seen a huge field of corn or another crop and wondered how long it took to harvest the food. Maybe you have wondered how people make toys, cars, phones, or other goods. Early manufacturing and farming was done by hand, and nothing was done very quickly. Many jobs were dangerous or difficult for human workers. Repetition could cause workers to lose concentration and injure themselves.

In response, engineers invented devices and machines that make jobs easier and faster. One example is the combine harvester. This machine does several things at once as it harvests plants. It replaced harvesting by hand.

Robots like this one can do huge amounts of farming work in just a few hours. The same amount of work would take a person a very long time.

Robots are important in manufacturing. Robots handle materials on production lines and assemble parts. They glue, paint, sand, and polish. They take the place of humans in **hazardous** areas. They can do work and clean up without putting humans at risk. Robots with powerful cameras can inspect and measure parts. They also choose and pack products in a warehouse. You probably own something that was produced with the help of a robot.

DELIVERY ROBOTS

Ready for a robot delivery? Starship Technologies created an on-demand package delivery system in some parts of the United States. When a package arrives at your address and you aren't home, you can instruct a Starship robot to deliver it to wherever you are.

This Starship robot is delivering food and drinks to users on a college campus in Virginia.

I deliver to Patriots
starship-gmu.com

STARSHIP

Robotics is important in farming too. Robots are designed for tasks such as picking, sorting, and packing. They can also do weed control, mowing, seeding, and plant maintenance.

Some can inspect vegetables and fruit for ripeness. Farmers use robot technology to increase production and save money. Farmers are also exploring robotics as a way to deal with labor shortages.

A BUSY BEE

The RoboBee, developed at Harvard's Wyss Institute, is a flying microrobot that could possibly be used for crop pollination and search and rescue missions. It could also possibly be used for weather, climate, and environmental monitoring. The RoboBee could work individually or within a group.

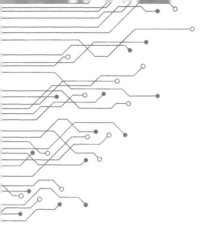

MILITARY AND CONSUMER ROBOTS

By air, land, and sea, military robots can do things that are too dangerous or difficult for soldiers. Bomb squad robots are used to locate and dispose of explosives and other dangerous weapons. They can also assist soldiers by carrying heavy equipment or performing other tasks.

Remote control guides most military robots. Some can respond to voice commands. These robots can search areas before soldiers go into them, keeping them safe. Robots using **artificial intelligence** (AI) might someday make it so human soldiers don't go into the battlefield at all.

The BigDog robot, made by Boston Dynamics, can walk where military vehicles are too large to go. It can carry up to 400 pounds (about 181 kilograms) and run 20 miles (about 32 kilometers).

You might not realize it, but you have probably interacted with a robot lately. Robots have a place in everyday life. Robotic vacuum cleaners can clean floors while no one is home. Different robots can be used to mow lawns or wash windows.

A robot mows a lawn so a human doesn't have to. An assistance robot in a grocery store (at right) monitors an aisle to help customers.

SCANNING IN PROGRESS

They can even be used in stores to help customers. For example, a robot can warn a customer about a spill or other tripping hazard while alerting the grocery store staff.

Robots can also keep track of what items are in a store and how much they cost.

EXPLORATION ROBOTS

When you picture a space explorer, you probably think of special suits. That's because humans cannot survive outside Earth's atmosphere. But robots do not have this problem in a space environment. Robotic equipment can explore moons and planets for us.

Robots give scientists information about our solar system and beyond. The Mars rovers began exploring Mars in 1997. They move around on the planet, keeping track of how the planet looks and collecting pieces of rock and other matter for scientists to study.

ROBOT TEACHER

The Crew Interactive Mobile Companion (CIMON) was designed to use AI to help astronauts. It answers questions and gives instructions as astronauts carry out experiments. CIMON is the first robot with AI to be tested in space.

NASA's Curiosity rover took this selfie on May 12, 2019 (the 2,405th Martian day, or sol, of the mission). This rover helps scientists study the climate, geology, and even the possibility of life on Mars.

A robot called Hedgehog can hop and tumble over rough planet surfaces. The Pop-Up Flat Folding Explorer Robot (PUFFER) can make itself flat and get into tight spots. Other robots can explore underneath icy surfaces on both Earth and other parts of the solar system.

Robots can gather data to help scientists learn about these unexplored places. This keeps scientists safe and helps them learn more.

Most rovers don't work upside down. The Hedgehog robot can work no matter which side faces up.

Exploring underwater has also changed because of robot technology. Human divers cannot dive deeper than about 131 feet (about 40 meters) because it is not safe for them. Remotely operated vehicles (ROVs) can dive much deeper and use special cameras and lights to explore the dark ocean.

ROVs help scientists learn more about the ocean. They can also locate shipwrecks and photograph deep-sea life.

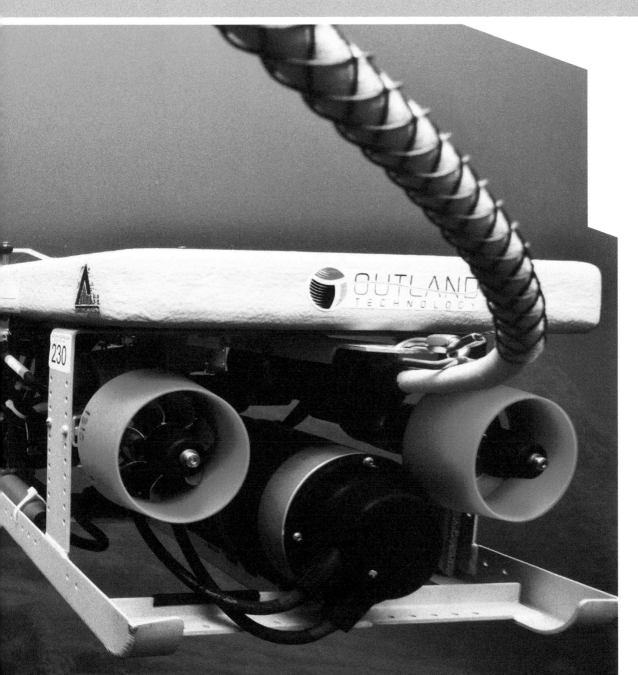

Other kinds of undersea robots work to map the ocean floor. Some marine robots even collect ocean garbage. The next time you see the ocean on TV or in person, just think: There could be robots out there!

ROBOTS TO THE RESCUE

Surgeons often do operations that require steady hands and excellent eyesight. A surgeon can use robotic devices to perform complex surgeries safely and with good results.

Robots are being developed that can do the jobs of nurses and medical assistants too. They can prepare medicines and deliver them to a patient's room at the hospital. Robots can even help doctors visit with patients many miles away.

Robots can also serve as patients. **Humanoid** robots are used to train students in dentistry as well as other medical fields.

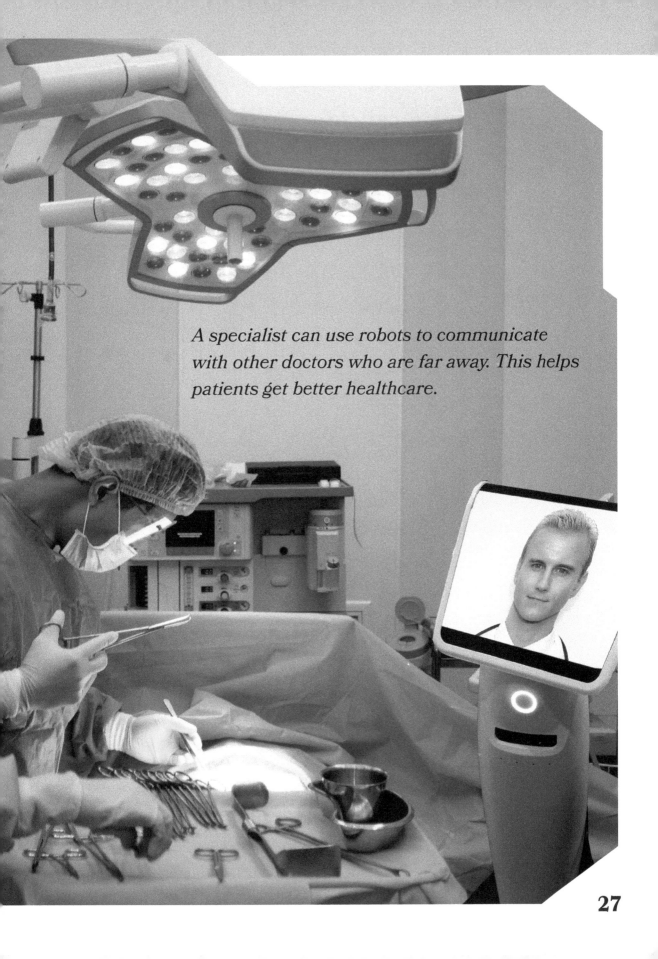

A specialist can use robots to communicate with other doctors who are far away. This helps patients get better healthcare.

Robots play an important role during disasters as well as in search and rescue (SAR) operations. Tiny robots can search through rubble after a hurricane or earthquake.

Following a disaster, robots can take photos and guide rescuers. Drones or unstaffed aerial vehicles (UAVs) are remote-controlled robots that can be used to fly over an area where it is too dangerous or difficult for people to go. They are also used to locate lost victims in places where it is difficult to travel. Robotic devices can deliver food, equipment, and medical supplies too.

Robotic firefighters are being developed to assist human firefighters. They can survive the extreme heat of a fire and pump water much faster than a human can.

Robots are changing the way we do many things. Thanks to robots, we are developing a safer, cleaner, and more efficient world.

SMART DRONES

An onboard computer powers many rescue drones. These drones are loaded with sensitive equipment including scanners, video cameras, and **infrared** cameras that can identify disaster victims.

Robots can help fight fires without putting humans in danger.

GLOSSARY

artificial intelligence (ahr-tuh-FISH-uhl in-TEL-i-juhns): the science of making computers do things that previously needed human intelligence, such as understanding language

automaton (aw-TA-ma-tahn): a robot that can operate on its own

autonomous (aw-TAH-nuh-muhs): existing or acting separately from other things or people

hazardous (HAZ-ur-duhs): dangerous or risky

humanoid (HYOO-muh-noid): looking or acting like a human

hydraulics (hye-DRAW-liks): machines that work on power created by liquid being forced under pressure through pipes

industrial (in-DUS-tree-uhl): related to making things

infrared (in-fruh-RED): producing or using rays of light that cannot be seen and that are longer than rays that produce red light

mythology (mi-THAH-luh-jee): a collection of myths

robotics (roh-BAHT-ihks): the science of creating and using robots

INDEX

TEXT-DEPENDENT QUESTIONS

1. What is a robot?
2. Why is it a bad idea for people to do repetitive tasks?
3. How have robots helped space exploration?
4. Why do we need a robot that can fight fires?
5. What are three things that underwater robots do?

EXTENSION ACTIVITY

Think of a task that could benefit from the use of robots. Draw a picture of a robot assisting with this task. What is it doing? Describe any ways that this robot might help humans in this role. Think of a name for your robot.

ABOUT THE AUTHOR

Robin Koontz loves to learn and write about everything from abalone to ziggurats. Raised in Maryland and Alabama, Robin now lives with her husband in the Coast Range of western Oregon. She especially enjoys observing the diverse wildlife on her property. You can learn more on her blog at robinkoontz.wordpress.com.

© 2020 Rourke Educational Media

www.rourkeeducationalmedia.com

PHOTO CREDIT: Cover ©Praphan Jampala; Pg 1 ©Visual Generation, ©Sergei Dubrovskii; Pg 4 ©Album / Alamy Stock Photo; Pg 5 ©Andrei Stanescu; Pg 6 ©Marsyas; Pg 7 ©Wiki; Pg 8 ©Wiki; Pg 9 ©Library of Congress; Pg 10 ©Scharfsinn86; Pg 11 ©Album / Oronoz/Newscom; Pg 12 ©Factory_Easy; Pg 13 ©Library of Congress; Pg 14 ©kung_tom; Pg 15 ©Wyss Institute for Biologically Inspired Engineering at Harvard University; Pg 17 ©JP5\ZOB/Newscom; Pg 18 ©Martin Wahlborg; Pg 19 ©Ekkasit919; Pg 20 ©NASA; Pg 21 ©NASA/JPL-Caltech/MSSS; Pg 22 ©NASA, Federico Rossi; Pg 24 ©Tane Casserley/NOAA; Pg 27 ©MONOPOLY919; Pg 28 ©Photomontage

Edited by: Tracie Santos
Cover and interior layout by: Kathy Walsh

Library of Congress PCN Data

Invention of Robotics / Robin Koontz
(It Changed the World)
ISBN 978-1-73162-981-4 (hard cover)(alk. paper)
ISBN 978-1-73162-975-3 (soft cover)
ISBN 978-1-73162-987-6 (e-Book)
ISBN 978-1-73163-334-7 (ePub)
Library of Congress Control Number: 2019945509

Rourke Educational Media
Printed in the United States of America,
North Mankato, Minnesota

CPSIA information can be obtained
at www.ICGtesting.com
Printed in the USA
BVHW090226210522
637141BV00001B/8